The Nested Bowls

The Promise and Practice of Good Governance

by
Laura Park

Unity Church-Unitarian
St. Paul, MN

ISBN-13: 978-0692149478
ISBN-10: 0692149473
Unity Church-Unitarian Publishing

For more information about governance systems and how your organization can benefit from governance consultation, please visit unityconsulting.org

Editing by Ellen Green
Book design by Shelley Butler

Published by Unity Church-Unitarian
732 Holly Avenue
St. Paul, MN 55104
651-228-1456
www.unityunitarian.org

Acknowledgments

This book would not exist without the courageous and generous leaders of Unity Church-Unitarian. For ten years, they've allowed me to develop and hone my practice of these skills with them, challenging my assumptions, and asking for more depth. I am particularly grateful to Rev. Rob Eller-Isaacs and Rev. Janne Eller-Isaacs who, early in their ministry with the church, along with Barbara Hubbard, Executive Director, took a risk on an unknown congregant who wanted a capstone project for her master's degree in organization development, and then championed the process that emerged from that project. Their spiritual guidance has been transformative.

I am also indebted to the leaders of the many congregations who have worked on this process with me over the years. Every time I do this with another group of leaders, I learn something new to improve the approach.

The kind hearts and keen intellect of my Unity Consulting colleagues, Joe Sullivan and Rev. Roger Bertschausen, have also added greatly to the process and approach.

I am deeply grateful to Linda Mandeville and Ellen Green who carefully read and edited early drafts of this work. I am indebted to Shelley Butler for her insightful comments on later drafts and for her generous and expert navigation to publication. There would be no book without her.

Finally, I must acknowledge my patient husband, Erik Jordan, who over the years has been steadfast in his belief that this work was important and worthwhile. His support has made this work possible.

The Nested Bowls
The Promise and Practice of Good Governance

Table of Contents

Chapter One
Awaken Compassion. Transform Lives. Bless the World.

For the last ten years, I've worked as a congregational governance consultant for Unity Consulting, a program of Unity Church-Unitarian in St. Paul, MN. I get puzzled looks when I tell people what I do, and I find people usually appreciate the clarification of my elevator speech. "What I really do," I say, "is help congregations identify their purpose, the difference they make in people's lives, and then I help them organize to deliver on that promise."

At Unity Consulting, we liberate and empower the leadership of progressive religious congregations and other institutions so that they can awaken compassion, transform lives, and bless the world. Our work on governance starts with a step we call Casting the Vision. Congregations and institutions that make a real difference in the world first articulate the core values that guide all their work, the mission that flows from those values, and the more specific differences in lives that will advance the mission. These values, mission, and ends statements fit together like nested bowls, each building upon the other to ground the work of the congregation in shared purpose and meaning.

This is primary board work and the board must earn the right from its sources of authority and accountability to discern and articulate these Nested Bowls. It needs to have an intentional, systematic, and comprehensive conversation with the congregation and other sources of its authority and accountability about their values and their vision of the congregation's future. Only then will the board have the data it needs to authentically do its Nested Bowls articulation.

It's challenging to have a conversation like this that inspires and connects its participants, that begins with people's lived experience and builds to a shared vision of the future that's desired, bold, affirmative, and grounded. This book is the user's manual for that work. It outlines

1

a conversation process that's inviting and connecting, and then describes how to take the data that emerges from that process to fill the Nested Bowls.

Boards using this process:

- Ask and answer powerful questions about how the congregation is meant to be in the world and what it's meant to create for the world.
- Earn the authority to answer these questions through deep and meaningful conversation with the congregation as a whole—and potentially other sources of the board's authority and accountability.
- Develop the ability to serve as a source of prophetic imagination to the congregation about its future.
- Lay the foundation for a fruitful governance practice that keeps the congregation focused on its mission.

Many trustees experience this work as the deepest and most meaningful of their time on the board, work that gives structure and purpose to their legal and fiduciary roles. This work develops board service into a shared spiritual practice, one that connects board service to the holy and creates a ministry of governance that helps the congregation put first things first.

This book can benefit both lay and professional congregational leaders but is particularly focused on the lay leaders of the board and their needs and their work in this process. The board's role in leading the congregation through a process of mission discernment is both crucial and often outside their comfort zone. It asks the board to govern the congregation with prophetic imagination, not merely manage its operations. Most lay leaders find this asks for new skills, and this book shows them how to embody those skills as they navigate this process.

This work is spiritual and religious, and the next chapter explores its theological roots. In addition to these roots, we owe a debt at Unity

Consulting to John Carver and Policy Governance®.[1] Unity Church-Unitarian embarked on a governance transition in 1992. Its board of trustees and minister were looking for a more effective way to relate to one another and to articulate and fulfill the mission of the church. They found the essentials they were looking for in John Carver's Policy Governance® system.

Policy Governance® provides a systematic way to ground the work of the congregation in its core values and to organize power and authority for visioning and decision-making in alignment with those values. The questions Policy Governance® asked the congregation to answer—and the clarity the method provided about who answered which questions in what way—liberated and empowered leadership in the congregation for its mission and ministry.

At the same time, the leadership of the church noticed the need to translate and interpret Policy Governance® for congregational life. This book provides that interpretation as it applies to the discernment and articulation of values, mission, and ends. If you're familiar with Policy Governance®, you'll recognize the ways in which our approach is informed by Carver's work. If you're not familiar with Policy Governance®, you'll still be able to follow our approach and find value in it.

Future books about the work of Unity Consulting will address how we help congregations organize to deliver on their promise of the difference they'll make in people's lives. This book will help you think creatively and deeply about why your congregation or institution is in the world, and subsequent books will help you align your organizational life with your purposes, and to be specific, strategic, and accountable in pursuit of your stated ends. We begin with the material in this book, however, because it lays the foundation for everything else fruitful governance makes possible.

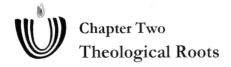 Chapter Two
Theological Roots

Progress is now seen not to take place through inheritance; each generation must anew win insight into the ambiguous nature of human existence and must give new relevance to moral and spiritual values.
—James Luther Adams, *Guiding Principles for a Free Faith*

Only a move from a managed world to a world of spoken and heard faithfulness permits hope.
—Walter Brueggemann, *The Prophetic Imagination*

Two 20th-century theologians particularly inform the principles of free association and prophetic imagination on which this process is based: James Luther Adams and Walter Brueggemann. Five key themes from their writings inform the process outlined in this book: freedom, covenant, justice, criticism, and hope.

Freedom

Freedom in this context is not the libertarian freedom to do whatever we want, but the freedom that comes from and is grounded in our faith in and our connection to something deeply creative and larger than ourselves. The ability to speak prophetically to a future that envisions and builds the Beloved Community rests on our ability to acknowledge an ever-changing, creative force that exists beyond our control but that has our confidence and loyalty nevertheless. As James Luther Adams puts it: "…we must depend upon a transforming reality that breaks through encrusted forms of life and thought to create new forms. We put our faith in a creative narrative that is re-creative. Revelation is continuous."[1] This is his first "smooth stone" of religious liberalism.

Walter Brueggemann says that an understanding of God's freedom is essential to the prophetic voice: "The point that prophetic imagination must ponder is that there is no freedom of God without the politics of justice and compassion and there is no politics of justice and compassion without a religion of the freedom of God."[2]

This connection to a transforming reality that grounds a living faith tradition is at the heart of the process this book discusses, and deeply informs its structure and what happens with its outcomes. The process begins with a connection to the holy, to that free spirit freely moving, and moves from there to invite the congregation to consider a Powerful Question about its future. This conversation process helps the board to, in theologian Martin Buber's words, "Listen to the course of being in the world…and bring it to reality as it desires."[3] The process acknowledges change and ambiguity, our individual communication with and connection to a creative God, and what that connection means for us when we come together into covenanted community.

 ### Board Reflection: Question on Freedom

Throughout this book, you'll find exercises inviting your board to reflect on and deepen the information provided in the chapter, to take you through the process this book outlines. Some exercises introduce a topic and ask the board to consider its own ideas and understandings before addressing the material in the chapter itself. Some exercises invite the board to try out the information in a chapter to develop the process for its own use and deepen its understanding of what follows. This chapter offers board reflection questions to deepen your understanding of the theology on which this process is based. Use them one at a time as check-in questions for board meetings or consider them all at once for general board development.

How have you seen the freedom of continuous revelation do its work within your congregation?

Covenant

The theme of freedom extends from our individual relationship to God to our relationship with each other, and to the promises we make to one another as we are in relationship to one another. James Luther Adams' second "smooth stone" of religious liberalism says that "all relations between people ought to rest on mutual, free consent and not on coercion"[4] and "the method of free inquiry is the necessary condition for the fullest apprehension of either truth or justice, and also for the preservation of human dignity."[5]

Walter Brueggemann speaks of covenant as the promises made between a personal God and a community. He speaks of covenant as fresh, renewing, life-giving, and hopeful, which is very much aligned with the energy James Luther Adams finds in covenant. Brueggemann says that "Promise belongs to the world of trusting speech and faithful listening"[6] which is the world this process of congregational conversation about mission works to create.

What's powerful in these views of covenant is the vibrancy of freedom and change that they both embody. Because we freely associate with one another, because we listen carefully and deeply to one another, because we can make and re-make our promises to one another, this enables prophetic speech and prophetic imagination and that enables our work for justice and our reason for hope in a broken world. This vibrancy and purpose from free connection is built into this process of mission discernment and thus into congregational governance as a whole.

Martin Buber says that human beings are the promise-making, promise-keeping, promise-breaking, promise-renewing animal. It's these promises, these covenants, that give shape and meaning to our lives together in community. The process outlined in this book helps us name these promises for congregational life in ways that keep them in front of us, so that we make sure we keep them and renew them when we, because we are human, inevitably break some of them.

Board Reflection: Question on Covenant

In what ways has a life-giving, spirit-renewing sense of covenant operated in your congregation?

Justice

James Luther Adams' third "smooth stone" of religious liberalism "affirms the moral obligation to direct one's effort toward the establishment of a just and loving community. It is this obligation which makes the role of the prophet central and indispensable in liberalism."[7] Both Adams and Brueggemann call us to *act* for justice and note that justice emerges from a free people freely connected to one another and to a free God. And it is the prophet who pushes us to both find and act for justice.

Adams says:

> The reign of God, the reign of the sustaining, transforming reality is the reign of love, a love that fulfills and goes beyond justice, and love that cares for the fullest personal good of all. This love is not something that is ultimately created by us or that is even at our disposal. It seizes and transforms life, bringing us into a new kind of community that provides new channels for love and new structures of justice.[8]

If our congregations are to be this new kind of community, if we are to be the alternative community that Brueggemann envisions, where the prophetic voice counters the numbness of the larger culture and enables us to act to create goodness in the world, we need to think about what governance structures will enable that continually new creation. As Adams says, in his fourth smooth stone of liberalism, "The creation of justice in community requires the organization of power."[9]

This asks us to think about how the board finds its own prophetic voice, how it expresses it, how it partners with its minister to bring the congregation's power to bear to allow that sustaining, transforming reality to act to create justice. The process in this book enables the board to do that work.

This process, and our belief that the lay leaders of the board can effectively lead it, is also grounded in James Luther Adams' understanding that the church is the priesthood and prophethood of all believers. We are all capable, are all tasked, with developing our ability to criticize and energize for good. Prophets, Brueggemann says:

> are completely uncredentialed and without pedigree so they just rise up in the landscape...they imagined their contemporary world differently according to that old [covenantal] tradition [of Moses]. So it's tradition and imagination...they are moved the way every good poet is moved to have to describe the world differently according to the gifts of their insight...people who control the power structure don't know what to make of them, so they characteristically try to silence them.[10]

Our process invites the board to be the prophets, so that the congregation's power structures are aligned with its future possibilities.

 Board Reflection: Question on Justice
How has your congregation heard the call to act for justice, grounded in the spirit of transforming reality? Who are your prophets, and where have they emerged?

Criticism and Hope

Two final themes relate to the prophetic imagination of the board and the way we've designed this process: criticism (or lamentation) and hope. They go together, because together they engage and serve the new reality that's seeking to emerge.

James Luther Adams focuses primarily on hope in the way he phrases his fifth "smooth stone" of religious liberalism. "Liberalism holds that the resources (human and divine) that are available for the achievement of meaningful change justify an attitude of ultimate optimism."[11] But Adams also acknowledges that "there are ever-present forces in us working for perversion and destruction"[12] and says that liberalism denies this at its peril. "The optative mood alone offers only a truncated, and, in the end, frustrated conjugation; the full paradigm demands the penitential and imperative moods as well."[13]

Adams' insistence that we combine hope with humility and exhortation is resonant with Brueggemann's insistence that the prophetic voice first engage with criticism or lamentation, particularly because of the nuance he brings to the understanding of prophetic criticism. This is criticism that "consists not in standing over against but in standing with; the ultimate criticism is not one of triumphant indignation but one of the passion and compassion that completely and irresistibly undermine the world of competence and competition."[14] Brueggemann says that "Quite clearly, the one thing the dominant culture cannot tolerate or co-opt is compassion, the ability to stand with victims of the present order. It can manage charity and good intentions, but it has no way to resist solidarity with pain or grief."[15]

The prophetic voice does not stay in grief, does not only criticize, does not retreat to nihilism as Adams puts it. Instead we have an obligation to bring our resources to bear on the future with hope that we can make things better. "Progress," says Adams, "is now seen not to take place through inheritance; each generation must anew win insight into the ambiguous nature of human existence and must give new relevance to moral and spiritual values."[16] It's Brueggemann who gives us the practical way to engage with one another to find anew those insights and the relevance of moral and spiritual values when he says that

"Only a move from a managed world to a world of spoken and heard faithfulness permits hope."[17]

The process in this book is all about that spoken and heard faithfulness. That process helps the board learn the current relevance of the church's moral and spiritual values and put what it discovers into policy that guides everything the congregation does. In following the process in this book, the board engages in compassionate criticism that stands with people, not over them, and finds its way to hope that the church can make a difference in the world.

 Board Reflection: Question on Criticism and Hope
What expressions of criticism and hope exist in your congregation? How have they guided your congregation and its sense of purpose?

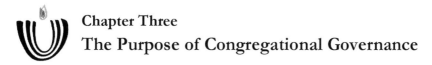

Chapter Three
The Purpose of Congregational Governance

It is madness to wear ladies' straw hats and velvet hats to church; we should all be wearing crash helmets. Ushers should issue life preservers and signal flares; they should lash us to our pews.

—Annie Dillard, *Teaching a Stone to Talk*

 Board Exercise 1
What's the Purpose of Governance?

This exercise invites the board to consider its own ideas about the purpose of governance.

Before your next board meeting, ask every trustee to review board agendas, meeting minutes, board policies, and other documents. Notice what questions the board considers. Notice how your board invests its limited time.

- What do these documents say about the current meaning and purpose of governance in your congregational system?
- What is the current job of the board and its trustees?

Discuss the members' answers to these questions at a board meeting. How satisfied is the board with the current purpose of governance in its congregational system?

We begin with the purpose of governance, because it deeply informs how we structure our process for mission discernment. Here's our provocative proposition: The purpose of fruitful governance is to liberate the energy and creativity of the congregation to awaken compassion, transform lives, and bless the world. Boards that serve this purpose serve as a source of the congregation's prophetic imagination, enabling a "priesthood and prophethood of all believers"[1] to come together to "listen to the course of being in the world and bring it to reality as it desires."[2]

How often does the board serve that purpose? If yours is like most church boards, not often enough. The boards beginning work with us more often say they spend their time second-guessing decisions that other, more qualified people, better connected to the issues at hand, have already made.

Or they simply ensure that everyone has signed off on a decision before it is implemented, making it difficult if not impossible for the congregation to launch any exciting or challenging projects that respond nimbly to current conditions or needs. Or they consider unimportant questions while an unelected shadow board makes the real decisions about the future of their church.

Boards starting work with us often say they rarely consider questions of the church's relevance, impact, meaning, or purpose. And when they do, they don't come to powerful conclusions because the congregation doesn't have clearly established systems of accountability and authority for answering those questions well or for making the reality they envision come to fruition.

We have a video of imaginary before-and-after board meetings that we use to illustrate this dynamic.[3] In the video, trustees consider how to make up the church's regularly recurring budget deficit. They talk about what's been tried before, about how tired everyone is of asking for money. They talk about small measures they're taking to avoid spending and to raise money. At the end, they ask for a report that will postpone action on the problem.

Conference attendees laugh as they recognize the activities of the "before" board. Clearly, they have experienced times when their boards became mired in the details, disconnected from the larger purpose for which their congregations exist.

The "after" board meeting has a much different energy. The church still faces a budget deficit, but the minister and the lay leaders working to secure the church's financial health provide a report to the board detailing the steps being taken to resolve the immediate problem. The board knows there's work still to be done, but it's confident the reporting group recognizes the issues and is addressing them operationally.

This frees the board to consider the larger questions of purpose that could be feeding the ongoing issue. The members use board time to map out a strategy to connect with the people who can help them better understand the extent to which they've been successful in moving their mission forward. Realizing that people contribute financially to a mission that's relevant and inspiring, they reach out to those who can help them imagine how they might deepen their church's purpose and make it more compelling.

Imagine a governance system with the energy of this "after" board, one that asks the board to engage with bigger-picture questions of the church's future. Imagine a governance system that lays a foundation of clearly articulated purpose for everything the congregation does, that aligns the congregation's resources to its purpose, and that asks for accountability in creating a world imagined in community. That's a governance system grounded in prophetic imagination, one that liberates and empowers leadership.

Building a governance system like this may require you to shift some of your basic assumptions about church and the use of power within it. Here are the five key assumptions at the foundation of our practice:

Assumption 1: Church matters.

What we do within, among, and beyond our congregations saves lives, literally. It matters that we do church well; it matters that we fulfill our core purpose.

Church done well helps us discover and connect to something larger than ourselves, something that will endure beyond us. Church done well wakes us up, helping us to discover and connect with life's meaning and purpose. Church done well breaks our hearts open and organizes the compassion that rises to do good in the world.

In this amazing and broken world, how can we afford to settle for church that does anything less?

Assumption 2: Churches need good leadership.

Because church matters, it matters that we find and can keep good leaders capable of steering our congregations to fulfill their purposes. We must establish systems that invite good leaders to emerge and help them thrive. We must use their time and their talents as fruitfully as possible so that they can make it possible for our churches to live into their promise.

Assumption 3: Good leadership emerges and thrives when given clear outcomes and clear boundaries.

One congregation embarking on governance transition demonstrated this in a powerful way: The board chair taking over midway through the transition found her way back into leadership because she could see that the congregation was finally getting clear about who was to make what decisions and within what parameters. She was excited about the powerful questions given the board to consider on behalf of and in conversation with the congregation, both during the transition and afterward.

She could see the new system enabling her to apply her leadership talents in the best interest of the church as a whole, because it clearly established the sources of authority for the board's decision-making, it provided tools for accountability, and it established covenant between the board and the congregation and between the board and the minister.

Assumption 4: The primary function of congregational governance is to liberate leadership for the church's mission.

This means that boards cannot afford to spend time making, reviewing, or rehashing decisions made by paid and volunteer staff. This wastes the energy and leadership of people who are in a better position, with better information, to make and implement effective decisions.

Instead, effective congregational boards focus their time with laser-like intensity on the questions and decisions only the board can make on behalf of the congregation. They:

- Know their sources of authority and accountability and work to get and stay in touch with them as they do their work so that their decisions are in the best interest of their sources as a whole.
- Define desired congregational outcomes in terms of what difference the congregation exists to make and in which people's lives. In this way, they create a unifying vision of the congregation's larger purpose, releasing great

creativity for the means of fulfilling that
purpose.

- Define the boundaries of prudence and ethics
within which the congregation must do its
work.
- Regularly consider whether their congregation
is making effective progress on changing
people's lives as articulated in their outcomes.
- Regularly assess whether the congregation is
honoring the boundaries of prudence and ethics
they've established.
- Clearly delegate the rest and then step back to
let others lead.

Assumption 5: Accountability is part of the deal.
A board liberates the energy and creativity of its church
leadership not for just any purpose but rather to fulfill
the purpose of church. That means it must ensure
accountability for outcomes.

How well has our church advanced its mission? Did we
in the congregation and on staff honor our values in
the process? What's the next question to consider
about the congregation's mission and purpose?

This is part of what makes governance covenantal. We
make promises to one another, and we find out
whether we've kept them, so that, if we haven't kept
them, we can renew our promises and begin again in
love.

How does board practice change under these assumptions? The board
lifts its vision beyond the perpetuation of the church as an institution,
beyond keeping everyone happy, beyond keeping the church stable,
beyond day-to-day operational issues. It focuses instead on how the

church makes a difference in people's lives and how best to articulate a compelling purpose for the church as a whole. And it works to ensure that the resources of the church are aligned with making that difference.

The board focuses on relationships in a different way. It stops being the court of last resort as it moves from management to governance. It stops responding to the loudest or the most insistent or the most complaining voices. Instead, it defines and commits to a governing relationship with the congregation as a whole that informs the board's visioning work. It commits to a governing relationship with the ministers and staff that liberates their energy and creativity for the mission of the church.

A board that governs well knows how its governing role adds value to the congregational system. It brings the talents of all board members to bear to fulfill that role well. This is incredibly important for churches that want to respond nimbly to a rapidly changing culture and society. Effective governance sets appropriate parameters, establishes powerful outcomes, and gets out of the way so that as many people as possible can participate in advancing the congregation's mission.

One of our partner consultants, a minister who led his midwestern congregation through two decades of steady membership growth, saw the impact effective governance can have on a congregation. Clarity about roles, about who made which decisions, and about mission and outcomes contributed to the congregation's ability to welcome new members and shift congregational culture as it grew from 150 to more than 750 members. Growth was not the purpose of the church, but as it pursued its purpose, it grew, and good governance was a crucial element that made graceful growth possible.

This is governance that knows what comes first and puts first things first so that second things can follow. Discerning what comes first starts with the question: Whose are we?

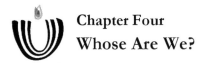

Chapter Four
Whose Are We?

The moment when, after many years
of hard work and a long voyage
you stand in the centre of your room,
house, half-acre, square mile, island, country,
knowing at last how you got there,
and say, I own this,

is the same moment when the trees unloose
their soft arms from around you,
the birds take back their language,
the cliffs fissure and collapse,
the air moves back from you like a wave
and you can't breathe.

No, they whisper. You own nothing.
You were a visitor, time after time
climbing the hill, planting the flag, proclaiming.
We never belonged to you.
You never found us.
It was always the other way round.

—Margaret Atwood, "The Moment"

Board Exercise 2
Whose Are We? Part I
Trustees' Sense of Accountability

This exercise helps your board consider its own ideas about authority and accountability in governance.

Before your next board meeting, ask each trustee to reflect on these questions:

- When you said yes to board service, on whose behalf did you accept this call?
- To whom are you accountable as a trustee for your work?
- To whom is the board accountable for its work?
- From whom does the board receive its authority for its work?

Open your meeting with trustee reflections.

The moment Unity Church-Unitarian's board recognized to whom it really belonged, the moment it identified the true source of its authority and accountability, was the moment it began a journey of transformation and discovery that influenced every aspect of congregational life.

Before its governance transition in 1992, the board's trustees tended to represent constituencies within the church. The nominating committee worked to ensure that someone on the board was involved in and could advocate for each of the church's program areas—religious education, community outreach, music, finance, facilities, and the like. Board meetings involved conflict and compromise among these constituencies. The trustees rarely glimpsed the larger whole to which all areas contributed.

This was particularly true because the board felt responsible for managing, if not actually doing, the work of the church and its ministries. Had this board considered the questions in Board Exercise 1 about the meaning and purpose of governance, it would have answered that its purpose was managerial. The board reviewed decisions made by others and made decisions no one else felt authorized to make, particularly those involving more than one program area.

The time spent tending to this managerial work made it difficult, if not impossible, for the board to consider the larger whole to which all areas contributed, to consider the larger meaning and purpose of the church's work.

The new governance system asked the board to consider its function in the congregational system from the perspective of a larger accountability. The board's governance work asked trustees to look beyond their responsibility to themselves or to a particular church constituency and instead consider their responsibility to the church as a whole. The board considered that larger accountability through a series of questions:

- In whose best interest do we work?
- Whose voices do we have no moral right to ignore?
- Whose values and vision are we accountable to representing as a whole?
- Who should influence what our future will hold?
- Who should tell us whether we're on the right path, whether we're creating the future we're meant to be creating?
- Who cares about and invests in the future of our congregation beyond the benefits they receive from it?
- Who validates the governance work we do?

The board decided that its answer to these questions was the congregation's members. As the congregation's legal owners and the people who have invested in the congregation beyond the benefits they themselves will receive, the congregation's members, as a whole, represented the board's source of authority and accountability.

The board's standard for judging its work became how well it effectively and authentically represented the values and vision of the congregation's members and their best interests as a whole.

This new standard for its work meant the board had to make room for an entirely new task: systematic, intentional dialogue with the congregation's members, asking them to put on their ownership hats and inform the board about the big issues facing the congregation. As John Carver puts it, "Governance is not management one level up; it is ownership one level down."[1] The board is not there to manage the congregation's affairs. The board is there to make sure the organization is aligned with the owner's values and vision.

Connecting with the congregation at the level of values and vision requires a shift in perspective. The board is not asking about people's satisfaction with church programs. It's not responding just to the people who happen to speak or just to the loudest voices. It's not presenting information or making a report (at least, not as a primary purpose). Instead, the board asks a broad cross-section of people in the congregation about their real, lived experience and how it connects with what they value about the church.

The board asks them to describe a future for the church where the best parts of the past are expanded and developed. It asks about possibility and growth: What could we build together on the strengths of our past? The trustees listen carefully to the answers.

And then the board discerns what is at the heart of all the feedback it has received: What are people telling the board about the central purpose of the institution and the difference in lives it's called to make?

Of course, that Unity Church-Unitarian's board identified the congregation's members as its source of authority and accountability does not mean that the board listens only to the congregation's members to determine the church's direction. To represent the members' best interests effectively, the board also must be widely connected to a number of people and deeply informed from a number of information sources, including the congregation's ministers and staff, its neighbors, other congregations, and the wider faith. When it comes time to make a decision based on the information the board has gathered, however, the question it works to answer is: What's in the best interest of our congregation's members as a whole?

Notice that this question—what's in the best interest of our congregation's members?—doesn't ask for consensus or a vote. It asks for discernment: If the congregation's members had all the information that the board has (including the information gathered directly from the members), if they were able to discuss this issue at the depth the board has been able to discuss it, what would they decide was in the best interest of the group as a whole?

Discerning which people are the source of the board's authority and accountability, discerning which people are the board's owners, means that the board must distinguish owners from:

- Stakeholders—those affected by the actions of the congregation.
- Beneficiaries—those receiving services or benefits from the congregation.

While the board gathers information from stakeholders and beneficiaries to inform its work, it articulates the future based not on particular stakeholder and beneficiary interest but on the best interest of its ownership as a whole.

This gets complicated in congregations because congregants can be owners and stakeholders and beneficiaries at different times. Congregants talking to the board about their religious values and their vision for the future of the church are acting as the board's source of authority and accountability—as owners. Congregants who live near the church and are affected by the church's decisions about its property are stakeholders. Congregants talking with the minister about the church's religious education or the content of the worship service are speaking as beneficiaries. This means that the board must systematically and intentionally connect with congregants as owners, in dialogue specifically about the values and future of the organization.

The answer to the question of whose we are—our congregation's members—served the board well for several years, uniting trustees in common understanding about the proper focus of their work.

That understanding began to shift, however, as the congregation considered its connections beyond its walls and realized the impoverishment of disconnection from people in the wider community who shared its values, but were not members because of divisions of culture, race, and class.

What, the board wondered, might be the implications of that impoverishment for governance? Might the board find an answer to the whose-are-we question that would include people beyond its walls as sources of authority and accountability? An answer that would insist on the board engaging in a regular, systematic practice of connecting to these people and using what it learns to inform choices about the church's future?

Unity Church's board, as part of its governance transition, had developed a practice of regularly reviewing and renewing its policies, so when this policy came up for review, the board considered whether a new answer to "Whose are we?" might make sense. As trustees reflected on the current answer—the congregation's members—they saw how that definition encouraged self-perpetuation. The board continually connected to the people already there. The board wanted to find a definition capturing the connection missing in its previous definition.

The board decided that the theology of Beloved Community might have something to offer its definition of ownership. Over the next six months, trustees read and reflected on readings, sermons, and other resources on Beloved Community. They asked themselves:

- How do we understand the phrase Beloved Community?
- What does Beloved Community mean theologically? What does it call us to be and to do?
- How might the board incorporate an understanding of Beloved Community into its definition of its sources of authority and accountability?

At the end of the study, the board changed its definition of its sources of authority and accountability. Where before the moral ownership of Unity Church-Unitarian was identified as its members, the definition now reads: "The moral owners of Unity Church-Unitarian are those who yearn for the Beloved Community and see Unity Church as an instrument for its realization. The Beloved Community is engaged in the work of the spirit. It is community at the highest level of reality and possibility, where love and justice prevail."

You'll notice this definition uses the term *moral owners*. In Policy Governance®, that term broadens the board's sources of authority and accountability beyond the legal owners to others from whom the board wishes to derive authority and to whom it wishes to be accountable. Connecting the concept of moral ownership to Beloved Community helped Unity Church's board encompass all those to whom it felt an obligation to be in accountable relationship in determining the future of the church.

Changing its definition of ownership changed the way the board approached its work of systematic, intentional connection with its ownership. For example, building on connections established by the church's ministers, the board hosted a dinner and conversation with religious leaders from traditionally African American congregations in its near neighborhood, to begin to understand their values and their faith and what they were building for the future. The board then considered how their values and their work to change lives might intersect with the board's decisions about how Unity's work could change lives.

The board also designed an extensive process to listen to members of the church's Community Outreach Partners so as to inform its articulation of the church's future *(see* Chapter Six: Earning the Authority to Articulate the Nested Bowls). Trustees talked with staff, volunteers, and service recipients from these organizations, asking about their vision of the community they were trying to create and using their responses to help the board articulate outcomes for the church over the next five years.

Redefining the board's sources of authority and accountability influenced not only the board and its work but also the operational side of the congregation. It catalyzed a larger "opening" of Unity Church to the neighborhood around it. As one former board member put it, "We began to look in a much more intentional way about our larger responsibility and opportunity in the world—especially in our own backyard." One example of this is board Policy J, holding the Executive Team accountable for assessing the church's vendors on their justice and sustainability efforts.

Two other important examples:

- The Executive Team reflected on the way in which the church's building allowed congregants to welcome and connect with all those who yearn for the Beloved Community and launched an award-winning remodel of the church to open it more effectively to the community.
- The church now shares its worship space with an African-American neighborhood congregation, Above Every Name— "an emerging cutting edge ministry . . . created to be a 'Church for the People' . . . a place where God's Creation can Relate, Receive, and be Released to experience the unending measure

of God's Love, Mercy, and Grace."

> If the board hadn't changed the definition of the church's ownership, the congregation might not have done the work making it possible to welcome this partnership that has been rich for both congregations.

The board's conversations around moral ownership were some of the deepest it's ever had. The change in moral ownership policy asked the board and the congregation to consider who they are, who they want to be, and how their accountability can hold the institution to a larger vision. The process of revising this policy asked the congregation to step up to a larger expression of faith and be accountable to it.

This is the experience of a board asking itself the powerful questions of good governance: Six months of study led to two new sentences of governing policy... and everything changed.

There are no shortcuts to this depth. It asks for patience and courage and the wisdom to know which is called for in which moment. Patience for the right moment to begin a new conversation, patience with process when the outcome isn't clear, patience with congregants wondering whether the board contributes anything by writing two sentences of policy after weeks of research and conversation. And courage to initiate new growth and new ideas, again where the results may not be completely clear and particularly when the board discerns that its choice may be in the best interest of its moral owners though those owners might not yet choose it.

The board of the Unitarian Universalist Association (UUA), the organization of covenanted Unitarian Universalist congregations, has particularly demonstrated both comfort with ambiguity and the courage to introduce new ideas. The UUA board defines its Sources of Authority and Accountability[2] as:

1. Our member congregations
2. Current and future generations of Unitarian Universalists

3. The heritage, traditions, and ideals of Unitarian Universalism
4. The vision of Beloved Community
5. The Spirit of life, love, and the holy

You'll notice that some of its Sources are not immediately identifiable as people. Our experience is that the boards of many congregations and religious organizations working to understand their larger accountability find themselves coming up with more abstract definitions of their Sources of Authority and Accountability. The challenge, of course, is how to be in dialogue with such abstract sources as the "vision of Beloved Community."

As we worked with the UUA board on how to operationalize its Sources, to give definition and clarity to the voices representing its Sources and then to get and stay in touch with these Sources, the connections clearly added depth to the board's deliberation. Each Source added a distinct perspective to the question of the organization's future direction. Being clear about who spoke as a Source and who did not, made it easier for the board to discern the best interest of the Sources overall and to have the courage to follow that path.

Answering the question "Whose are we?" asks the board of a religious organization to begin its work in humility and service, acknowledging the limitations of individual trustees and the board as a whole and centering its governance practice in the human longing to be connected to that which is larger than ourselves and will endure.

Each congregation, each institution, will come to a different articulation in answering that question, but since governance is all about authority, accountability, and the appropriate use of power, fruitful governance practice begins with the board defining which people hold its accountability. The answer holds the board's most important covenant: to act in accordance with the best interest of its sources of authority and accountability as a whole.

Board Exercise 3

Whose Are We? Part II

Defining Your Sources of Authority and Accountability

This exercise helps your board apply the information in this chapter and define its sources of authority and accountability.

To define your board's sources of authority and accountability:

- Consider trustee reflections from Part I of this exercise. Use those reflections to create a list of categories of people to whom you sense accountability, from whom you get your authority to act. Particularly consider your larger accountability: Whose are you?

- Consider who might come off this list of potential sources. Whose needs would you take into account without necessarily making your decisions in their best interest? These are stakeholders—people affected by the work of your congregation or religious organization but not the ultimate source of the board's authority or accountability.

- Group your potential sources. Which sources are similar and might be defined together?

- Will one definition of your sources serve well, or do you need a list?

- Define in writing your sources of authority and accountability.

Chapter Five

What Belongs in Our Nested Bowls of Values, Mission and Ends?

There's a thread that you follow. It goes among
things that change. But it doesn't change.
People wonder about what you are pursuing.
You have to explain about the thread.
But it is hard for others to see.
While you hold it you can't get lost.
Tragedies happen; people get hurt
or die; and you suffer and get old.
Nothing you do can stop time's unfolding.
You don't ever let go of the thread.
> —William Stafford, "The Way It Is"

We shall not cease from exploration
And the end of all our exploring
Will be to arrive where we started
And know the place for the first time.
> —T. S. Eliot, from "Little Gidding"

Board Exercise 4
Current Definition of Values, Mission, Ends

This exercise helps the board consider its own ideas about values, mission, and ends.

Three questions for board discussion:
- How does our congregation currently define its core values, its mission, and its ends/goals/outcomes?
- How well are our values, mission, and ends known in our congregational community and beyond it?
- In what ways does our congregation align its work to its values, mission, and ends?

Once the board understands its bedrock relationship with its sources of authority and accountability, it's ready to build a connection with them that will allow it to authentically establish the foundation of a fruitful governance practice. We've come to use a metaphor of "Nested Bowls" of values, mission, and ends and to use the question "What belongs in our Nested Bowls?" to guide this work. The graphic shows the powerful question posed by each of the bowls in our Nested Bowls metaphor and how the bowls fit together.

THe nesTeD BOWLS

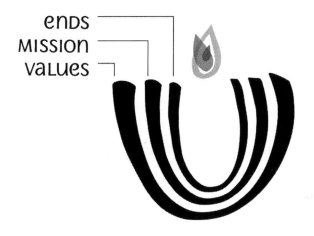

 enDS
MISSIOn
values

VaLUeS What transcendent, timeless qualities of our religious community will we embody in all we do?

MISSIOn What is our transcendent purpose—what overarching difference are we here to make and for whom? Whose lives will we change and in what way?

enDS What more specific, measurable differences will we make and for whom?

 **sources OF auTHoriTy anD accounTaBiLITy**
(THe FLaMe THaT LIGHTS THe BOWLS)

Whose are we? How can we get and stay in touch with our sources of authority and accountability, including, but not limited to, our members?

These are big and abstract questions, and you may find it challenging to see their relevance to the "real" work of governance—the questions of fiduciary responsibility, of how to organize and control the organization, particularly its finances. But effective boards align all their governance work with their answers to the questions of the Nested Bowls. It's not possible to make effective choices about how to organize roles within your congregation or how to control your congregation's finances without first knowing what values your organizational and financial choices need to align with or what difference in people's lives your organizational and financial choices exist to create in the world.

You may also think your congregation already knows the answers to the Nested Bowls questions. But unless you have clearly articulated answers that have been refreshed/revised within the past five years and to which your leadership consistently refers in its work, it's worth taking the time to answer the Nested Bowls questions in conversation with the congregation—before moving on to other governance work. This is particularly true if your congregation is like Unity Church-Unitarian, where 20 to 25 percent of its members have joined within the last five years.

Religious organizations and congregations in particular need the grounding provided by the Nested Bowls articulation, since these institutions seek to unite individuals, each on a unique spiritual journey, in community and common purpose. What makes that merging of individual seeking and common purpose possible is a clear and compelling articulation of the promises that bind the community together, the promises about what the community will create in the world. The Nested Bowls ask us to be clear about those promises, so that we don't get lost in institutional self-perpetuation or in turf wars that don't serve our larger purpose. A board that's done its Nested Bowls work is better positioned to perform its fiduciary work with authority and authenticity, in alignment with the congregation's purpose.

Let's look more closely at the Nested Bowls questions and what it means to answer them.

Values

The first bowl, the largest bowl, is the values bowl, and the values bowl question is:

> *What transcendent, timeless qualities of our religious community will we embody in all we do?*

This is a question of both current condition and of aspiration, one asking us to know both who we are and who we want to be.

We encourage congregations to choose no more than five, and ideally three, words or short phrases capturing the unique mix of qualities the congregation seeks to make real in the world. These words are often nouns—not nouns like *children* or *music* but rather nouns like *courage* or phrases like *broad, open embrace* that evoke the overarching qualities the congregation aims to embody.

These are the first and most important choices a congregation makes in determining its direction, and the conversations that inform those choices are rich and inspiring. Some of the questions boards consider as they discern the congregation's core values are:

- What does it mean to choose a particular word like *transformation* or *integrity* or *relationship* or *wonder* or *becoming* as our religious community's core value?
- How do we understand the meaning of each word we choose?
- How are the words we choose more meaningful than other synonyms we might choose instead?
- How do we see all the words we choose becoming a package embodying the unique qualities of our congregation that we wish to live into?

Of course, no board can answer these questions without conversation with the congregation and the board's other sources of authority and accountability to inform its work. Boards working to articulate the congregation's core values first must engage in a process that anchors the core values it chooses in the energy and experience of its sources as a whole and particularly in the spiritual life of the congregational community as a whole. For the congregational conversation, we use an exercise called "The Experience of the Holy."

Several assumptions ground the creation of this exercise. If you share these assumptions, this exercise should be useful to you as well. They include the beliefs that:

- Each individual's unique spiritual experience matters when building a religious community.
- All are called to speak their truth and be heard.
- The strength of a religious community rests in its ability to unite and expand individual experiences of the holy.
- A congregation's core values must reflect its unique place in people's religious and spiritual lives. The congregation's core values must be grounded in what's holy to the people in the community.

You'll find this exercise, and how to use the data it provides to discern core values, described in Board Exercise 5.

Board Exercise 5
The Experience of the Holy

This exercise helps your board gather the data it needs to articulate the congregation's core values.

This exercise asks participants to share a time when they experienced the holy.

Most congregations find they must state what they mean by an "experience of the holy" so that it aligns with their theology and the congregation's culture. Some congregations ask people to think of a time when they experienced a connection with God. Some ask people to think of a time when they experienced a connection to something larger than themselves, a time when they felt their hearts and minds expand. Make sure your understanding of what it means to have an experience of the holy is clearly communicated when you introduce the exercise.

Do this exercise as a board to understand how your experience of the holy informs your religious values. Then do it with your congregation as a whole to help the board discern the congregation's core values.

Partner up with someone in the room. Take five minutes and tell your partner about a time when you experienced the holy, a time when (insert your understanding of this experience here). Take another five minutes to listen deeply to your partner's story. Give your partner the gift of your undivided attention and deep understanding. Don't interrupt except to encourage her or him to continue the story. Don't use their story to launch your own ("That reminds of a time when I . . ."). Make sure your partner feels deeply heard.

After you've both told your stories, talk about the values that undergird them. What qualities of the experiences were key to their being holy? What words or very short phrases describe those qualities? Did your stories speak to a quality of courage or openness or freedom or authenticity or respect or humility or . . .

Take five minutes to make a list of all the values words or phrases that relate to your stories. Then, take five minutes and choose THREE words or very short phrases that BOTH of you would want to pull forward into the future of your religious community. Five minutes isn't a lot of time, so don't agonize over your choices. Tap into your intuitive knowledge of yourself, your partner, and your religious community. Go deep quickly, talking about what really matters to both of you right away.

Then join another pair. Share your lists of three values words, and take eight minutes to choose THREE values words or short phrases ALL FOUR of you would want to pull forward into the future of your religious community. Again, don't agonize. Tap into your intuitive knowledge, and go deep quickly. Write the three words on a piece of flipchart paper.

Each group of four will then share its list. What do you notice about the words people chose?

Once you've done this exercise as a congregation, bring all the lists together. What words are said most frequently? How would you group the words into similar ideas? What words particularly resonate with the stories board members heard as the congregation did this exercise? As you discuss the answers to these questions, gradually reduce the values words until you have just three to five that are at the core of who you are and who you want to be.

Here are some examples of core values established by congregations with whom we've worked:

Unity Church-Unitarian values:

- Authenticity
- Generosity of spirit
- Mutual respect
- Freedom of thought
- Open, broad embrace

Congregation One values:

- Inclusion
- Compassion
- Engagement
- Human responsibility
- Celebration

Congregation Two values:

- Transcendence—to connect with the wonder and awe of the unity of life
- Community—to connect in sorrow, joy, and service with those whose lives we touch
- Compassion—to treat ourselves and others with love
- Courage—to live lives of honesty, vulnerability, and beauty
- Transformation—to pursue growth that changes our lives and heals our world

Notice how one gets a different understanding of each congregation's culture from its core values. Notice how one congregation added a short, descriptive phrase to its core values. This was particularly valuable for a word like *courage*, whose meaning in this context is slightly different from the usual definition.

You may wonder how such lofty words could be useful in guiding a congregation's work. At Unity Church, the values of authenticity, mutual respect, and open, broad embrace remind members to connect with people outside the church walls whom they might not already know. The intent to live into these values was part of the catalyst for broader discussion of its moral ownership highlighted in Chapter Four.

This broader understanding of its moral ownership eventually led to a capital campaign raising far more than thought possible for an award-winning remodel of Unity Church's building to better integrate with its neighborhood. A lot depends on the strength of the foundation laid by the core values.

Mission

The next bowl in the Nested Bowls metaphor—the bowl that rests inside the values bowl and whose contents flow from it—is the mission bowl.

The mission bowl questions are:

> *If we live fully into our values, what is our transcendent purpose?*
> *What overarching difference are we here to make and for whom?*
> *Whose lives will we change and in what way?*

To illustrate the power of expressing your congregation's mission as an answer to these questions, let's look at some examples.

Unity Church-Unitarian:

> The mission of Unity Church is to engage people in a free and inclusive religious community that encourages lives of integrity, service, and joy.

Notice that the "for whom" in this mission statement is *people*. That's an intentional choice. Rather than say that the congregation exists to make a difference for congregants, the choice to make a difference for people calls the church community into ever deeper relationship with people its members do not yet know and have not yet welcomed into relationship.

Expressing the mission in this way asks members to consider which people have access to the community and how it might broaden its reach and appeal. It also asks members to consider what it means for people of all types and backgrounds to engage with the religious community—and to implement a variety of means to encourage lives of integrity, service, and joy.

Just one example of this is the Circle of Peace Movement, which sponsors a circle meeting at Unity Church every Monday night. Started by coworkers of a church member (who are now church members themselves), the group brought together warring neighborhood families in a safe, neutral place to share a meal and talk in circle about how to end neighborhood violence and promote racial healing. The church's mission both encouraged this group and allowed its support by the church.

Many congregations we work with are finding mission statements that coalesce around three verbs to express the impact the church has on lives in the church community and beyond. Here are two examples.

Congregation Three Mission:
> In the Universalist spirit of love and hope, we give, receive, and grow.

Congregation Four Mission:
> Living with integrity
> Nurturing wonder
> Inspiring action

Notice how these mission statements identify a change in the lives of the people in each congregation. But they also imply an ultimate impact on people beyond the walls in the action catalyzed in their members. These missions are broad, but deliberately so, to allow a wide interpretation of what the action verbs mean and to encourage efforts to advance the mission and make it real.

Notice, too, that none of these mission statements reference programs or activities. Mission statements that answer the question of the mission bowl don't talk about what the congregation *provides*. They don't even mention worship.

This is part of the power and the challenge of the mission bowl question—it asks the board to look beyond a congregation's activities to the larger picture of how those activities transform lives. This, in turn, opens a world of possibility for activities that live into the mission and allows leaders throughout the congregation to apply their resources and creativity to moving the congregation toward the realization of its mission.

Having a mission statement that answers the questions of the mission bowl also gives congregants a larger perspective on their church's purpose, reminding everyone that the church exists not for the sake of its own perpetuation but to change lives. This helps everyone change and grow to respond to changing times.

Finally, you'll notice that these are not small dreams. Missions aren't meant to be easy to achieve. The mission is meant to serve a congregation for the long term, to stretch it, to serve as a beacon of possibility. It is a call to the future that inspires continual effort and constant renewal and reinterpretation.

Ends

The ends question relates to the mission question but at a finer level of detail:

> *What more specific, measurable differences will we make and for whom?*

It's not enough to have a mission—you must live it. As times change and your understanding of your mission changes, a more current, more specific expression of the difference your congregation makes in people's lives keeps your mission alive and relevant. Nesting ends inside of mission, using a question but with a more specific and measurable focus, gives the mission a current, relevant focus and direction.

We recommend that congregational boards attach a time frame of about five years to their ends, a period during which the congregation will work to fully realize its ends. Every year during that time frame, the board assesses what progress the congregation has made in making its ends real. At the end of that time frame, in conversation with the congregation and the board's sources of authority and accountability, the board refreshes its answers to the ends bowl question. In this way, the board renews, reinterprets, and reconnects to its congregational mission, giving it new life and meaning.

Five years may seem like a long time to have ends in place, particularly when these are meant to be more specific and measurable differences in lives. But congregational ends, because they're about equipping people to live lives grounded in their faith and values, are still broad and transformational. Congregations need sufficient time for church programs to take hold and create the difference in people's lives that their ends identify.

Many people ask us whether they can call the ends bowl by some other, more familiar, name like goals, outcomes, or strategies. We always respond that it doesn't matter what you call the bowl, only that you answer the powerful question posed by the bowl. Using an unfamiliar term like *ends* (which we borrowed from Policy Governance®) is useful because it guides people to use the ends bowl question to understand what belongs in that bowl.

Some congregations have found that when they answer the question "what difference for whom now?" they benefit from an organizing structure that we call *within, among,* and *beyond*. What difference do you want to make *within* congregants as individuals, in their individual spiritual lives? What difference do you want to make in lives as you build religious community *among* congregants? And what difference do you want to make in lives *beyond* the walls of your congregation?

Unity Church-Unitarian uses the *within, among,* and *beyond* structure to organize its ends.

Ends Statements 2014–2018

Within

The people of Unity Church-Unitarian value a deeply meaningful, transforming liberal religious experience. As individuals, we:

a. Open ourselves to compassionate pastoral care in times of joy, sorrow, and transition.

b. Develop spiritual practices that nurture reverence and encourage diverse worship services rich in beauty, serenity, community, and joy.

c. Embrace our identity as Unitarian Universalists and live out the principles of our shared faith in our daily lives.

d. Cultivate a spirit of curiosity and welcome, growing from a desire for authentic relationship.

Among

Unity Church-Unitarian is a community of welcome, reverence, and deep connection. As a community, we:

a. Sustain and encourage one another in love.

b. Reach out to one another across differences and stand together in the face of injustice.

c. Value our shared ministry and practice it with integrity

d. Foster a culture of open, inclusive leadership and meaningful engagement.

e. Are generous with our time, talents, resources and creativity.

f. Are careful stewards of our resources and facilities.

Beyond

Unity Church-Unitarian carries out the work of love in community, making a positive impact in our neighborhood and in our world. Grounded in the transforming power of our faith, we:

a. Open our doors and our hearts to those who seek comfort, courage, and meaning.

b. Build authentic relationships with people across differences, in a spirit of humility and reverence.

c. Live out our commitment to racial reconciliation and to dismantling racism.

d. Serve as a trusted and visible leader, partner, and advocate for the creation of a just society and a sustainable environment.

e. Participate actively in the larger Unitarian Universalist community.

As you read through these ends, notice how they:

- **Establish a covenant and encourage covenanting.**
  By developing the ends through conversation with the congregation and other sources of authority and accountability (*see* Chapter Six: Earning the Authority to Articulate the Nested Bowls) and using the word *we,* the ends are established as a covenant among congregants to pursue certain commitments together, to change their own lives and the lives of others in the ways the ends identify.

  When considering the question of covenant, "What shall we promise to one another and in what interest?" the congregation looks to the ends to know the promises that give shape and meaning to their life together in a particular religious community.

  The ends also encourage covenanting as a verb, as a continuing practice of renewal. Jewish philosopher and theologian Martin Buber said that humans are the "promise-making, promise-keeping, promise-breaking, promise-renewing animal"[1] that finds meaning together in a continuous process of covenanting.

  Refreshing the ends every five years, working together to make the ends real, reflecting together on what progress has been made, renewing the promise of the ends when we fall short—all these are part of a religiously covenanted life together.

- **Encompass the whole of the congregation's ministry.**
  Though ends identify the specific and measurable outcomes that the congregation pursues over a particular time frame, they are still broad goals. If you find yourself tempted to write ends that result from just one part of the congregation's work in the world, you haven't thought broadly enough about how church changes lives overall. Everything that happens in the congregation—from worship to choir to religious education to community outreach work to administration—should be working to make all the ends real.

- **Fulfill a governing purpose.**
  As with mission, ends do not specify what programs or services the congregation will provide but instead identify what will change in people's lives because the church provides those programs and services well. This is a challenging change in perspective for most people. We're accustomed to thinking about what initiatives to start, what projects to develop—a new program for young adults, a remodeled kitchen, an educational initiative on systemic racism. What's far more difficult—and valuable—is to identify whose lives will be changed, and how, as a result of the congregation's existence. This is the work of governing as distinct from managing.

  Again, as Jim Brown puts it so well, "Governing is not management one step up; it's ownership one step down."[2] This means that identifying which results the ownership wants is the first step toward effective board service. Or as author and educator Stephen Covey says, "Begin with the end in mind."[3] This is also true of highly effective congregations.

- **Use the congregation's voice.**
  Some congregations, seeing that ends are broad and that writing their own may be daunting, wonder whether they might adopt ends from other congregations. We advise against this. A congregation wants to hear its own voice in the ends, with language authentically describing its strengths and possibilities.

44

Learn how to gather the data necessary to writing in the congregation's voice in "Chapter Six: Earning the Authority to Articulate the Nested Bowls."

- **Build additional detail through a nesting structure.**
  In Unity Church's ends, there's an overarching end for each category of *within, among,* and *beyond* and additional detail nested inside each category. Not all congregational boards choose to write ends this way, but it illustrates the importance of a board asking itself how much detail is needed to describe the future toward which it wants the congregation to move. The board always asks at what point its voice can stop and leave implementation to the operational leadership.

- **Incorporate a time frame for accountability.** Unity Church's board adopted its ends for a five-year time frame (2014–2018), which means those ends serve as the focus for the congregation's activity from 2014 through 2018. By the end of 2018, the board wants to say the ends are realized. The connection of these ends to a time frame and the commitment to see them realized are key to the congregation's accountability to the ends. The board's commitment is to monitor progress on the ends: Are the congregation's resources producing the results the community has covenanted to produce?

Knowing that you'll need to monitor progress on your ends makes it tempting to articulate ends that lend themselves to straightforward, precise assessment. Resist that temptation. As John Carver says, "A crude measure of the right thing beats a precise measure of the wrong thing."[4]

In *Good to Great and the Social Sectors: A Monograph to Accompany Good to Great,* Jim Collins says, "What matters is not finding the perfect indicator but settling upon a consistent and intelligent method of assessing your output results and then tracking your trajectory with rigor."[5]

As you articulate your ends, focus on discerning the difference your congregation truly and deeply wants to make in people's lives and trust that you'll find a consistent, intelligent, useful method of accountability in the next phase of your governing work.

Another reason to assign a time frame to ends is that it builds the responsibility to refresh them regularly. Religious communities grow and change. Assigning an endpoint ensures that the board will respond to change and the opportunity it brings. Plus it's important that a congregation's membership maintains a connection to the ends and has the sense that the ends reflect the community's shared purpose. As mentioned earlier, 20 to 25 percent of Unity Church-Unitarian members are new within the past five years, which means that if the ends are not refreshed every five years, a significant percentage of the membership will not have experienced or participated in the conversation establishing the ends.

Thus, even though a board may feel no need to change the ends after five years, it's critical to invest in a congregational process to refresh and potentially revise them. Every time Unity Church's board invests in this congregational conversation, it finds that the process of living into the previous ends has changed the church community and helped it to grow in depth and meaning. This means the board needs new ends to keep pace with that growth and better steer the congregation toward its possibilities.

Here are some additional examples of congregational ends to give you a sense of how flexible and adaptable this model is for governing. You'll notice that the numbers of the congregations are out of order. That's because some of them have been mentioned earlier in the values and the mission sections.

Congregation Four (*see* this congregation's mission on p. 39)
Living with integrity, we:
- Use our heads and our hearts to develop a deep understanding of our individual and collective values, ethics, and personal

theologies and to align our individual and community actions in witness to those commitments.

- Support each other in life and life's transitions with loving care, celebration, and gratitude.
- Engage in lifelong learning, utilizing reason in the pursuit of truth.
- Care for the earth and its rich web of life.

Nurturing wonder, we:

- Experience the transcendent that opens us to deep connection and life's expansiveness.
- Develop intellectual and spiritual personal practices that actively engage us with paradox and mystery.
- Invite the wider world to join us in our exploration of the unknown.

Inspiring action, we:

- Pursue justice and equality courageously through bold individual and congregational endeavors.
- Integrate joy and service.
- Develop leaders who shift the larger culture toward justice and compassion.
- Welcome and connect with people across differences of ethnicity, class, sexual identity, religion, politics, and education.
- Form partnerships beyond our congregation consistent with our mission and values.

Congregation Two (*see* this congregation's values on p. 37)
Congregation Two is an intentionally hospitable community where:

- All people are treated with respect and dignity.
- All people of goodwill are welcomed.
- People are supported in times of joy and need.
- People find connection with one another in fellowship.

- We are fully engaged and generous with time, treasure, and talent.
- We invite people of goodwill to find a spiritual home with us.
- We engage as UUs in public life.

Congregation Two nourishes souls and transforms lives by:
- Engaging and supporting one another in spiritual practice and growth.
- Providing worship, programs, and activities that awaken meaning and transcendence.
- Providing a caring, supportive, and safe place to rekindle the spirit.

Congregation Two witnesses to justice in our personal lives and beyond by:
- Practicing liberal religious values in the public arena.
- Empowering all people to access the richness of life.
- Providing leadership to the greater UUA community to expand the reach of our movement.
- Partnering with the interfaith community to live our shared values.

Congregation Five

Congregation Five is an engaged, sustainable faith community grounded in UU principles and values. It exists so that:

A. Spiritual Home

   People of all ages and backgrounds find a spiritual home in this supportive, affirming religious community.

B. Community

   People are loved, valued, and connected.

C. Spiritual Growth

   Seekers can pursue their spiritual growth and transformation within the context of the covenanted UU community.

D. Faith Formation

Children, youth, and adults experience and explore the wisdom that all religions have to offer and can express UU principles and values.

E. Generosity

Congregants experience a shared richness of love and spiritual growth, inspiring greater generosity of time, talent, and treasure.

F. Faith in Action

Congregants can fulfill the UU values of social and environmental justice, and community organizations experience Congregation Five as an active and dynamic partner in this work.

At What Cost or Priority?

If you've studied Policy Governance®, you know there's a question we've left off our ends bowl question: At what cost or priority? In other words, what should the results of the ends be worth, from a cost-efficiency standpoint or a relative-worth perspective?

Caroline Oliver, in *Getting Started with Policy Governance*, asks the question this way: "What is the standard that your board believes should be used to justify the value of your organization's results as worth the amount of resources that were devoted to producing them?"[6] The classic answers to that question in Policy Governance® can feel arcane and unhelpful in a congregational setting:

- At a level that justifies the funds invested
- In a manner that represents good value for money
- With a level of cost efficiency exceeding that typically achieved by other similar organizations

But as John Carver points out in *Boards That Make a Difference*, "Although putting a dollar value on changes in the human condition is not an easy task, we do so implicitly all the time."[7] So should we not consider the cost efficiency and relative priority of our congregational ends?

We haven't yet come up with an overall definition of cost efficiency we're happy with, but we have deeply considered the relative worth of congregational ends and whether there's any benefit to describing a relative worth in the ends. Should congregations say, for example, that 45 percent of the congregation's resources will be devoted to producing ends within, 25 percent among, and 30 percent beyond? Most boards with which we've worked have decided that their ends are of equal priority because the religious life requires an equal balance of within, among, and beyond.

This is a more profound statement than it initially may appear to be. At Unity Church-Unitarian, the board determination that its *beyond* ends had equal priority to its *within* and *among* ends called for reflection on the way the church invested its resources and the extent to which the ends were advanced in equal measure. As it considered these questions, the congregation realized it had significant work to do to fulfill the beyond ends to the same extent as within and among. And it began to look for ways to advance them more effectively.

The church applied for a grant to start its Community Outreach program, including the initial funds to hire a Community Outreach coordinator. The program deepened the commitment of many current members to the church, attracting and retaining many new members. This in turn enhanced the congregation's pledge base and allowed the church to sustain the program when the grant ended. When the church analyzed pledging according to participation in church programs, it found that people who participated in its Community Outreach programs were among the most generous pledgers.

Another congregation, in reflecting on the degree to which it invested in and advanced its *within, among,* and *beyond* ends equally, came to the same conclusion: That the church's fulfillment of its *beyond* ends lagged behind the fulfillment of its other ends. And it worked to develop its pledge base so as to budget for a minister of community outreach. In giving its ends equal priority, the board asked for deeper generosity from its members, asserting that this represented a worthwhile investment on the part of the members.

The answer to the question "At what cost or priority?" may be just a one-or two-sentence policy statement, but because the question requires deep reflection and has broad implications, we recommend taking the time to consider that question after you've written your ends.

Chapter Six
Earning the Authority to Articulate the Nested Bowls

> There is no power equal to a community discovering what it cares about.
> —Margaret J. Wheatley, *Turning to One Another*

Given the function of ends and the importance of collaboration and dialogue in most congregations, church boards are often unsure about their authority to answer the Nested Bowls questions on behalf of the congregation as a whole. What gives the board the right to discern and articulate these foundational governing policies?

We represent the answer to that question by the flame in the Nested Bowls. The board's authority to do its work comes from its intentional, systematic connection to the voices of its sources of authority and accountability. Before the board can answer the Nested Bowls questions, it must be in deep dialogue with its sources to understand their values and vision of the future. In the language of Policy Governance®, the board needs to do linkage work first.

Board Exercise 5 introduced "The Experience of the Holy" as one method of deep dialogue around values. You'll want to combine a values-discernment exercise like The Experience of the Holy with a process that helps members of the congregation talk about the way the church has made a difference in their lives in the past and what they envision possible for the church to create in the future. An adaptation of Appreciative Inquiry (AI) works well for that purpose.

AI is a process that uses people's stories of their peak experience with an organization to uncover its strengths and build on them for the future. To understand more about the assumptions on which AI is based and the approach in general, you can start with *The Thin Book of*

Appreciative Inquiry by Sue Annis Hammond. We recommend Appreciative Inquiry to inform the board's work because it:

- **Grounds discussion of the future in real, lived experience from the past and present.** You want people to talk first about their lived experience with or at the church before they talk about general ideas or principles for the congregation's future. In this way, you ground their comments about what the future might hold in the reality of the congregation's past and present. This keeps the conversation authentic and connected to real possibilities.

- **Focuses on strengths**, not to sweep problems under the rug but because it makes sense to build the future on past and current strengths. This focus keeps the conversation inspiring and avoids a rehash of previous pain. If your congregation is deeply wounded and unwilling or not ready to move on, however, consider a circle process or other healing process before you do linkage around the ends.

- **Enables the board to connect with the full range of its sources of authority and accountability.** Whatever process you create, you'll want to involve congregants from youths to elders, choir members and social justice activists, parents of children, and people with as many kinds of identity and ways of connecting to your church as possible. If your sources of authority and accountability extend beyond the congregation, you'll want to adapt your process to hear from them too.

- **Helps the congregation have a conversation with itself and connect with one another.** There are so many benefits to the board sponsoring a process for people to talk with and listen deeply to one another. You honor the diversity of experience and perspective that forms your community. You help people see the bonds that bring and keep them together in community. You help people experience the congregation as a place where they can find themselves and as a place much larger than themselves.

Surveys, interviews and other one-way communication methods may be helpful supplements, but the board realizes the most benefit from a process that asks its sources of authority and accountability to connect and exchange information with each other. As the observers of such a process, board members will understand at a much deeper level the values and visions that call the members of the congregation together and move it forward.

- **Develops congregants' understanding of ends and their governing purpose.** The board job of writing ends is a challenging one, and it's helpful when the conversations that inform their development also helps congregants understand how ends work. Given such understanding, they better support the board's efforts and know how their work in the congregation's ministries makes the ends real.

In adapting AI for congregational conversation about mission and ends, we start by asking congregational boards to develop a Powerful Question to guide the process development and focus the conversation. The term Powerful Question comes from the book, *The Art of Powerful Questions* by Eric Vogt, Juanita Brown, and David Isaacs. Available on the World Café website, it "explores the three dimensions of a powerful question—construction, scope, and assumptions—and then offers sample questions for focusing collective attention, finding deeper insight, and creating forward movement."[1]

For example, when it came time for Unity Church-Unitarian to renew and refresh its ends, the board first considered what it wanted to know. What topic, the board asked, if explored with the moral owners, would best help the congregation imagine and explore its future possibilities together?

As trustees considered possible topics in small groups, one board member shared how much a recent exploration of courage and vulnerability had meant to him, how influenced he'd been by social researcher Brené Brown's work on the topic. (Millions of people have watched her TED talks about this). The board realized that courage and vulnerability connected with many issues on which the congregation was working, and that they connected with efforts over the previous ten years to open the congregation to the world beyond its walls, to neighbors it did not yet know. Ultimately, the board settled on the question "What does it mean to be courageous and vulnerable together?"

The board then created a series of questions related to the Powerful Question for the congregation to answer. It started with an individual's lived, best experience and branched out to consider what that experience suggested was possible for the church's future. The board designed several different ways for congregants to engage with those questions, many involving conversation, but some using music, movement, plays, or films to spark a connection with the Powerful Question.

The Powerful Question also helped inform a process of connection with groups and individuals beyond the congregation who were sources of authority and accountability for the board. You'll remember that Unity Church's board identified its moral ownership as "those who yearn for the Beloved Community and see Unity Church as an instrument for its realization." Board members connected with several people and organizations who were working to build the Beloved Community and had a relationship with the church, including ministers from other churches, staff and other people served by the church's non-profit Community Outreach partners, and leaders of interfaith groups working in the urban area where the church is located.

Although the board did not ask these groups the Powerful Question directly (it seemed removed from their ongoing work), the questions they did ask were informed by it:

- How would you describe the community you long to see and live in? (What does it look like? Who lives there? What is happening?)
- What could be done in the next five years to help make that vision of community real?

Here are some other Powerful Questions congregations have used to guide their AI-based linkage work:

- Grounded in courage and wonder, what might we create together for the future?
- What could we build through deep connection: with each other, our faith community, our city, and the world?
- How do our spiritual journeys unite us? Where could our yearnings take us?

Board Exercise 6
What's the Powerful Question?

This exercise helps your board identify a Powerful Question that will guide the linkage work to inform its articulation of mission and ends. What question, if answered well, would best help the congregation imagine and explore its possibilities together?

As a whole board or in small groups of trustees, talk about the changes you've seen at your church over the past five years and about the moments that have been powerful to you and to others at the church. Talk about the themes of congregational life you want your linkage process to explore or reinforce.

As they emerge in this conversation, list topics that you could explore further with the congregation. List them as they come to you and then work to make them broader, so that they touch on all aspects of the church's ministry: within, among, and beyond.

If you work in small groups, come back together as a whole board and share the list of topics each small group has created. Choose two or three topics from these lists, or that emerge from your conversation about the lists, that seem to best invite the kind of deep and broad reflection you need for your linkage work. Assign one or two people to draft possible Powerful Questions aligned with these topics. Follow the guidelines in *The Art of Powerful Questions* to write questions that:

- Are open-ended, starting with *what* or *how*.
- Find an affirmative way to frame the issue that the question addresses. For example, one board started its conversation talking about all the upheaval it had experienced over the last two years, and how difficult it was to be facing more change. We reframed that to look instead at the possibilities

change opens up and how to discover the most desired possibilities.

- Delight and energize you.
- Lead the congregation toward creative possibility.
- Surface appropriate assumptions. Ask yourself what assumptions you see about your congregation, your congregants, your community, and the world in each draft question. Do you need to reframe a question to surface more appropriate assumptions? Many congregations today, for example, consider what cultural assumptions are built into their questions, and whether their question will resonate across cultures and embody the Beloved Community.
- Contain an appropriate scope, broad enough to encompass your congregation's ministry but not so broad that it has no relevance and meaning to your congregational community. World peace is probably beyond your congregation's reach, but peaceful connection within congregants individually, among the congregation as it builds its church community, and beyond the congregation in its immediate neighborhood is very much within its grasp.

Once your board subteam has drafted the Powerful Questions, come back together as a board to finalize the question that will guide your linkage work, using the same criteria the subteam used to draft them.

While Unity Church's linkage process used a variety of approaches (conversation, film, music, plays), the first time a congregation discerns and articulates mission and ends, it's best to keep the linkage process simple. We usually help congregations conduct a series of AI-based workshop conversations that bring congregants together in groups of

12-20 people to consider the future of the congregation. We start the workshop with "The Experience of the Holy" exercise for values discernment before moving into interviews in the same groups of four. Each person on the group of four shares:

1. A story of the church at its best, related to the Powerful Question.
2. Three wishes for the church's future, again framed in the context of the Powerful Question.

Once everyone in the small groups has shared a story and wishes and documented story highlights and wishes on flipcharts, the small group creates a visualization of the future, building on the strengths and wishes just shared. Which of those wishes does the group find particularly desired, bold, affirmative, and grounded in the congregation's strengths?

To help people understand the power of ends, we ask that their visualizations look ten years into the future, that they imagine the wishes they find particularly compelling have come true, and that they answer the question "How is our church changing lives now that these wishes have come true?"

Throughout the workshop, which is facilitated by volunteers from the congregation, board trustees wander and listen. They sit close to several groups and hear as many stories as they can. They sit among several groups and listen for common words and themes. They watch the room as a whole to see where the energy of the room is going. They make note of the times when the whole room turns to a particular idea and says something like, "Yes, that!"

Coming out of this process, the board has a wealth of data to use in discerning the answers to the Nested Bowls questions: trustee observations of the process, flipcharts with three values coming out of "The Experience of the Holy" exercise, flipcharts with story highlights, flipcharts with wishes, and the group visualizations of the future.

Trustees analyze the data for common themes and use the information to discern the answers to the Nested Bowls questions.

There are a number of ways to organize the data into themes. Since ends are often categorized within, among, and beyond (*see* p. 42), we often begin by categorizing the story highlights and wishes into categories of within, among, and beyond, assigning two categories if a highlight or a wish speaks to more than one aspect of the religious life. Then, you can see which category captures people's attention most in the past (story highlights) and which category most captures people's attention for the future (wishes).

We've also found it useful to further categorize the within, among, and beyond highlights and the within, among, and beyond wishes into more detailed categories. Again, this allows the board to see where the congregation's attention is focused as it talks about what's best about its past (story highlights), and where the congregation's attention is focused as it talks about what's possible for the future (wishes).

Categorizing the future visualizations is more difficult, since they usually envision several possibilities. Instead, we urge boards to hang up the images groups create, in a gallery for all to see, and to create a slide show with pictures of all the visualizations. Before the board meets on retreat to discern and articulate the Nested Bowls, trustees should spend as much time as possible with these visualizations, noticing patterns and connections between them, as well as particularly compelling ideas of what's possible for the future.

When the board and the minister meet together on retreat to answer the Nested Bowls questions, spend the first part of your time together with trustees sharing three key themes they notice in the data, and three values words they want to be sure the board considers for the congregation's core values. Use these focused lists to guide your final discernment of values, mission, and ends.

Participants tell us again and again how spiritual this process becomes for the trustees and the congregants who participate in it. As the board frames a Powerful Question to guide its linkage work, trustees reflect on which religious qualities it would benefit the congregation to expand within, among, and beyond the congregation. Congregants experience the great gift of being deeply heard as they reflect together on their individual and shared experience of the holy and the community's meaning and purpose. Trustees, as they reflect on the way in which the congregation can next make a difference in people's lives, experience the power of gathered religious community connected in common purpose.

Skills Trustees Need for Linkage Work

As you consider these exercises, you may wonder whether you have what it takes to do this linkage work well, to connect effectively to your sources of authority and accountability. If your board struggles to design and implement a linkage plan, you may consider several possibilities for getting the help you need. Of course, you could hire a consultant, but if you don't feel you have the resources to do that, perhaps one of your congregants has organization development or research design skills he or she would be willing to share with you.

Or start small. Just do "The Experience of the Holy" in small groups across the congregation and see what emerges. Then later have a conversation about your congregation at its best. See what that tells you about the strengths you have to build on in your congregation.

No matter how your board designs its linkage process, trustees will want to bring particular qualities to the work to ensure its success:

- **Comfort with ambiguity.** The best linkage processes carefully structure the interaction between participants but leave the outcome wide open. Trustees need the capacity to fully engage with the linkage process without knowing exactly what will come out of it.

- **Active curiosity.** This quality helps trustees set aside preconceived notions and be open to whatever insights and information they gather through their linkage work. People can tell when you're interested in what they have to say. Work to develop an open interest in the possibilities they present.
- **Discipline and commitment.** Linkage is hard work, and to reap its benefits, a board must stay with the process even when it doesn't know exactly whether and how it will add value to its governance practice. That means trustees need:
- **Faith.** Enlist the help of good people to help you design and lead a linkage process with integrity. Trust that it will deliver the insights you need to lead.

The Minister's Role in Filling the Nested Bowls

So far, we've focused on the role of the board in filling the Nested Bowls, because fruitful governance practice gives authority and accountability for the articulation of these foundational governance policies to the elected leaders of the board. Many people ask us what happens to the minister's prophetic voice in this process? Do ministers become one of many voices heard in the board's linkage work, or do they have a special role?

Your congregation's minister is a *prime informant* to the board in its visioning work. Ministers provide theological reflection and grounding as the board chooses a Powerful Question to guide its linkage work. They help connect the board to congregants who can help them design and implement a linkage process. As the board articulates the Nested Bowls policies, the minister provides a reality check on the implications of the ends.

Some questions ministers can help answer for the board:
- Is the congregation ready to make this mission and these ends real? What will that require from the congregation spiritually, emotionally, and financially?

- How well do the ends reflect the congregation the minister knows?
- How well do the ends reflect what the congregation's faith asks from its members as individuals and as a community?
- In what ways could the board's ends help the congregation deepen its faith and commitments?
- What concerns might congregants have about the ends the board is considering, and how might the board address those concerns after it has discerned that the ends are in the best interest of the church as a whole?

In addition, ministers often have language useful in capturing the ideas the board is reaching to articulate in the ends.

One example of the authentic interaction between board and minister in articulating the ends comes from Unity Church-Unitarian's choice to explicitly name its commitment to racial justice in its ends. One of its *beyond* ends now reads, "Grounded in the transforming power of our faith, we live out our commitment to racial reconciliation and to dismantling racism."

Arriving at the decision to name this particular focus to the church's justice efforts started when the board explored a larger understanding of its moral ownership, of its sources of authority and accountability (*see* Chapter 4: Whose Are We?). After the board studied the concept of Beloved Community and named as its moral owners "those who yearn for the Beloved Community and see Unity Church as one instrument for its realization," board and ministers discussed what commitment that policy meant the church should have to the neighbors the congregation did not yet know. Racism emerged from that reflection not only as the nation's founding wound, but also as the defining issue for the neighborhood in which the church was located. Coupled with the ministers' capacity for anti-racism work, the board felt ready to commit the church's resources to a focus on racial justice.

Another example of how the board's governance work can ground and transform a minister's work comes from a congregation considering its core values. The board conducted the linkage process described in this book, including "The Experience of the Holy" exercise for discerning core values. In this process, congregants consistently lifted up *wonder* as a quality they wanted to bring forward into the future. This surprised the minister, who had not heard people talk this way about the congregation before.

After further discussion, board and minister realized that the congregation had not been given the invitation to talk about their congregation in that particular way before. They agreed the data showed that wonder was a quality people wished the church to embody and decided that adding it to their core values opened up possibilities for the congregation's spiritual growth that would enrich the minister's work.

Ministers' interpretation of the ends, a crucial element in a cycle of accountability for making them real, and a process a future book will address, can also change how the board articulates them. One congregation's board had originally set as an end that the congregation would create a community of radical hospitality. As the minister described how she would lead the congregation to deliver on radical hospitality, describing the kind of church that radical hospitality would call the congregation to be, the board realized that was more than they were ready to ask for from their people and changed the phrase to *intentional hospitality*.

You can see from these examples how the Nested Bowls become part of the board's and the congregation's relationship with its minister. Through their articulation, the minister is far clearer about a congregation's aims for its ministry and can far more effectively collaborate with the congregation to create worship, shift ministries, and introduce programs to make the ends real.

Endnotes

Chapter One: Awaken Compassion. Transform Lives. Bless the World.
[1] The authoritative website for Policy Governance® created by John Carver is http://www.carvergovernance.com.

Chapter Two: Theological Roots
[1] James Luther Adams, *On Being Human Religiously: Selected Essays in Religion and Society*, ed. Max L. Stackhouse (Boston: Beacon Press, 1976), 14.
[2] Walter Brueggemann, *The Prophetic Imagination, Revised Edition* (Minneapolis: Fortress Press, 2001), 8.
[3] C. Otto Scharmer, *Theory U: Leading From the Future As It Emerges* (San Francisco: Berrett-Koehler, 2009), xiii.
[4] Adams, *On Being Human Religiously*, 14.
[5] Adams, *On Being Human Religiously*, 15.
[6] Brueggemann, *The Prophetic Imagination*, 65.
[7] Adams, *On Being Human Religiously*, 15.
[8] Adams, *On Being Human Religiously*, 16.
[9] Adams, *On Being Human Religiously*, 18.
[10] Walter Brueggemann, Interview with Krista Tippett, *On Being*, December 13, 2013.
[11] Adams, *On Being Human Religiously*, 18.
[12] Adams, *On Being Human Religiously*, 19.
[13] Adams, *On Being Human Religiously*, 19.
[14] Brueggemann, *The Prophetic Imagination*, 95.
[15] Brueggemann, *The Prophetic Imagination*, 91.
[16] Adams, *On Being Human Religiously*, 18-19.
[17] Brueggemann, *The Prophetic Imagination*, 66.

Chapter Three: The Purpose of Congregational Governance
[1] James Luther Adams, *The Essential James Luther Adams: Selected Essays and Addresses* (Boston: Skinner House, 1998), 186.
[2] Scharmer, *Theory U*, xiii. Quote attributed to Martin Buber.
[3] "Lighting the Leadership Chalice – Governance Part 6," September 1, 2012, video, 11:43, produced by UU University from content by Unity Consulting, posted by Central East Region, UUA. https://www.youtube.com/watch?v=IUulLHWoJjw.

Chapter Four: Whose Are We?
[1] Jim Brown, *The Imperfect Board Member: Discovering the Seven Disciplines of Governance Excellence* (San Francisco: Jossey-Bass, 2006), 155. Jim Brown attributes this quote to John Carver.
[2] Unitarian Universalist Association. 2009. "Unitarian Universalist Association (UUA) Governance Manual," Unitarian Universalist Association, last modified July 1, 2009. Accessed June 6, 2018, https://www.uua.org/uuagovernance/manual/process.

Chapter Five: What Belongs in Our Nested Bowls of Values, Mission and Ends?
[1] Scharmer, *Theory U*, xiii. Quote attributed to Martin Buber.

[2] Jim Brown, *The Imperfect Board Member*, 155.

[3] Stephen R. Covey, *The 7 Habits of Highly Effective People* (New York: Simon & Schuster, 1989), 103.

[4] John Carver, *Boards That Make a Difference, 3rd Edition* (San Francisco: Jossey-Bass, 2006), 110.

[5] Jim Collins, *Good to Great and the Social Sectors: A Monograph to Accompany Good to Great* (New York: HarperBusiness, 2011), 8.

[6] Caroline Oliver, *Getting Started with Policy Governance. Bringing Purpose, Integrity, and Efficiency to Your Board* (San Francisco: Jossey-Bass, 2009), 94.

[7] Carver, *Boards*, 100.

Chapter Six: Earning the Authority to Articulate the Nested Bowls

[1] Eric Vogt, Juanita Brown, and David Isaacs, *The Art of Powerful Questions*, The World Café, accessed June 7, 2018. http://www.theworldcafe.com/tools-store/store/

Bibliography

Adams, James Luther. 1976. "Guiding Principles for a Free Faith. Boston: Beacon Press." In *On Being Human Religiously: Selected Essays in Religion and Society*, by M.S. Stackhouse. Boston: Beacon Press.

Brown, Brené. 2012. "Listening to Shame." *Ted Talks*. March. https://www.ted.com/talks/brene_brown_listening_to_shame.

—. 2010. "The Power of Vulnerability." *Ted Talks*. December. https://www.ted.com/talks/brene_brown_on_vulnerability.

Brown, Jim. 2006. *The Imperfect Board Member: Discovering the Seven Disciplines of Governance Excellence.* San Francisco: Jossey-Bass.

Brueggemann, Walter, interview by Krista Tippett. 2013. *On Being* (December 13).

Brueggemann, Walter. 2001. *The Prophetic Imagination, Revised Edition.* Minneapolis: Fortress Press.

Carver, John. 2006. *Boards That Make a Difference, 3rd Edition.* San Francisco: Jossey-Bass.

Central East Region, UUA. 2012. *Lighting the Leadership Chalice -- Governance Part 6.* https://www.youtube.com/watch?v=IUulLHWoJjw.

Collins, Jim. 2011. *Good to Great and the Social Sectors: A Monograph to Accompany Good to Great.* New York: HarperBusiness.

Hammond, Sue Annis. 1998. *The Thin Book of Appreciative Inquiry, 2nd Edition.* Plano, Texas: Thin Book Pub Co.

Oliver, Caroline. 2009. *Getting Started with Policy Governance. Bringing Purpose, Integrity, and Efficiency to Your Board.* San Francisco: Jossey-Bass.

Scharmer, C. O. 2009. *Theory U: Leading From the Future As It Emerges.* San Francisco: Berrett-Koehler.

UUA, Unitarian Universalist Association. 2009. "Unitarian Universalist Association Governance Manual." *Unitarian Universalist Association.* https://www.uua.org/uuagovernance/manual/process.

Vogt, Eric, Juanita Brown, David Isaacs. 2003. *The Art of Powerful Questions: Catalyzing Insight, Innovation, and Action.* Burnsville, North Carolina: Whole Systems Associates.

Wheatley, Margaret J. 2009. *Turning to One Another: Simple Conversations to Restore Hope to the Future, 2nd Edition.* San Francisco: Berrett-Koehler.

Index

For more information about governance systems and how your organization can benefit from governance consultation, please visit unityconsulting.org

About the Author

 Laura Park would have been astonished to be told in college that she was going to be a congregational governance consultant. A double major in English and chemistry at Carleton College in Northfield, MN, Laura went on to design and deliver soft skills training programs for a large insurance company. The capstone project for her master's degree in organization development was to design a process for her church's board at Unity Church-Unitarian in St. Paul, MN, to have a conversation with the congregation about values and mission. She became captivated with a governance system that asked a board to do that kind of work, and after she served on the board and as interim membership coordinator for the church, she was asked to become Managing Director of Unity Consulting, the church's program that helped congregations with their governance.

Laura consults with congregations around the country, helping them understand their purpose, the difference they make in people's lives, and then helping them organize to deliver on that promise. An expert facilitator, Laura enables her clients to govern effectively and discover congregational governance as a ministry and spiritual practice. You can learn more about Unity Consulting at www.unityconsulting.org.

37355836R00046

Made in the USA
Middletown, DE
26 February 2019